Introduction

So long as there are men, there will be wars.[1]

- Albert Einstein

In January 2012, the President of the United States of America announced the new strategic guidance for the Department of Defense, titled *Sustaining U.S Global Leadership: Priorities for 21ˢᵗ Century Defense*. As the title alludes to, the defense priorities focus towards new future security concerns. The nation is in a critical juncture and the whole world is watching. The debates have already started in Washington, DC concerning the restructuring of the force and its strategic focus. Some politicians argue that this will weaken the influence that the United States has on the international community. Regardless of disputes, the United States cannot afford to get this wrong. As President Ronald Reagan once said, "we maintain the peace through our strength; weakness only invites aggression."[2] Civilian and military leaders must examine the nation's history of military reform, while simultaneously looking forward and ensuring America has the best-prepared fighting force to face the next threat. The question then is what does that balanced force look like?

In the 236 years of its history, the United States of America has fought the War of Independence, War of 1812, Mexican War, a Civil War, Spanish-American War, two World Wars, several minor wars, Korea, Vietnam, the Cold War and has become a world superpower. A closer look at history shows a trend that the United States has often found itself unprepared for war. This state of unpreparedness traces back to four main areas: too small of a peacetime force, delayed mobilization, absence of future planning towards next conflict, lack of coordination to recruit and equip the military.[3] Has the United States learned from history or will the nation continue to make the same mistakes in the 21ˢᵗ century?

The global landscape of the 21st century consists of a variety of multifaceted security challenges, from poverty stricken failed states with terrorists to cyber warfare causing physical destruction. Couple the fragile security situation with unstable economic conditions and the situation becomes increasingly more difficult. After a decade of war, the United States is revising its security strategy and implementing military reform in an attempt to reduce the size of its defense force and budget.

As the United States completes its withdrawal of combat forces from Iraq and prepares to complete its combat operations in Afghanistan by 2014, the Department of Defense must be readily postured to protect its national interests. The United States military increased the size of its personnel in 2007 to surge operations in Iraq and Afghanistan. The services must now drawdown their personnel to a financially supportable level because of the approved reductions in the 2013 Department of Defense budget. Debates continue that the reduction in force is a result of budget cuts, while others argue that there is no need for the excess and it is time to return to a balanced force. The idea of balance between military capability and fiscal discipline is a novel approach compared to the typical military cuts seen after major wars.

The civilian and military leadership need to put parochial partisanship aside and have a focused strategy that applies the lessons of our nation's past. This will ensure that the military is manned, trained, and equipped to face future contingencies across the spectrum of warfare. A thorough assessment of current and future threats must drive the defense strategy, not fiscal constraint. The combination of reducing the size and the budget of the military inherits a degree of risk, such as not being able to conduct simultaneous operations in separate regions that require a large military presence for an extended period of time. The United States can mitigate this risk through strengthening relationships with our allies and coalition partners to share the burden of preserving peace across the globe. The idea of other nations sharing this endeavor can help Congress avoid making across the board cuts without consideration of how that affects certain capabilities.

Historical Context

What I fear is not the enemy's strategy, but our mistakes.[4]

- Thucydides

During the early days of the United States, the capacity of a standing army or the means to finance one did not exist. An agency or process to collect taxes did not exist yet either. Many of the Founding Fathers had to pay for their own expenses while the served as a member of the Continental Congress.[5] Additionally, the citizens were reluctant to having a standing army because of the memories of the British Army's familiar under the direction of tyrant to suppress the people. A greater sense of duty and patriotism was found in a militia of armed citizens to defend their freedom. At the outbreak of the Revolutionary War, in April of 1775, the reality of the financial dilemma became critical. The funding issue was resolved when the Continental Congress relied on Benjamin Franklin and John Adams to ask France and the Netherlands for a loan, which was granted.[6] While this met the financial need of the Continental Congress, the civilian leadership still had to depend on the ill-prepared state militias. Eventually, the Second Continental Congress identified the need and established a Continental Army in June of 1775. Unfortunately, these men had "very limited experience with managing the kind of forces needed for such an action."[7] Previous fighting was done by militias usually engaged in small skirmishes instead of large force on force battles.

It was not until the Second Continental Congress 1777, when the state delegates established the Articles of Confederation. Article VI mandated for "every state shall always keep up a well-regulated and disciplined militia sufficiently armed and accoutred, and shall

provide and constantly have ready for use, in public stores, a due number of filed pieces and

tents, and proper quantity of arms, ammunition and camp equipage."[8] Congress directed the

responsibility to the states to recruit, train, and equip their defense force. They also faced the

challenge of managing the size, employment, and organization of this newly created army, much

like the United States Government faces today.

The trend of unprepared standing militias still existed as the early Americans faced the

British during the War of 1812. Apparently, the experience of the previous war was ignored

because the nation still had weak militias, needed a trained military, and the states disagreed

whether or not to have a large standing army to face the European threat.[9] The large standing

British army influenced immigrants to flee to the new colonies in America. Next was the

Mexican-American War in 1846 where the American Army was growing quickly, but lacked in

depth of officer leadership to offer competent staffs for commanders.[10] Some of the younger

officers of the Mexican-American War would later serve in senior positions during the Civil

War.

At the outbreak of the Civil War, both sides had some veterans but those in the rank and

file were untested. By 1861 at First Bull Run, the forces did not show much improvement of a

prepared military. In fact, a soldier from the 2d Wisconsin Infantry said, "it is safe to say that

not a man in the regiment knew anything of actual warfare, although none of the companies,

including mine, were organized from as many independent companies of state militia."[11] After

the Civil War, the United States really began its expansion of gaining additional territories to

support its population growth. Additionally, the nation became a larger stakeholder in the matter

of international relations, which opened up trade opportunities to boost the economy.

The beginning of the 20th century illustrates a period of transformation in tactics, professional military education and equipment for the United States military. The first test came when the United States entered World War I. America came to the assistance of their European allies to achieve victory, but at the cost of tens of thousands of American lives. A less than adequate institutional training program to pass on the experience from veterans to the new servicemen contributed of the high loss of life during the conflict. Many of the soldiers and Marines understood what needed to be done at the tactical level to defeat the enemy, however; those lessons learned were not captured or communicated to the service leadership in order to train the growing military. It was very much an on the job training scenario for many of the units on the front lines.[12] The retention of lessons learned varied among the services. The Navy and Marine Corps learned a great deal, while the Army experienced more difficultly incorporating the lessons learned because of its tremendous growth in personnel.[13]

The aggressive expansion of the services outpaced the capacity to provide quality combat training to the incoming personnel. The result was measured in quantity versus quality, which is consistent with a strategy of attrition. The size of the U.S. Army in 1915 was approximately 100,000 men strong and Army planners suggested that the U.S. would need a force between one and perhaps as many as 3 million men.[14] The decision to increase the size of the force so rapidly with the help of the Selective Service Act of 1917 included a mix of conscription, regulars, and the National Guard.[15] This approach only answered the need for quantity but lacked the quality. The war finally ended in the fall of 1918 as an Allied victory, which started the interwar period before the outbreak of World War II.

The military involvement of the United States through World War I ended victoriously but at a high cost of American lives. As the United States matures as a nation and the world stage changes, the 20th century consists of creative innovation in varied forms across the services. "In spite of low military budgets and considerable antipathy towards military institutions in the aftermath of the slaughter in the trenches, military institutions were able to innovate in the 1920s and 1930s with considerable success."[16] The next 20 years of peace gave the United States plenty of time to implement lessons learned for the government to fund the necessary growth and for military professionals to prepare for the next war.

The early years of the 20th century were formative years for the nation's military including individuals living in that era. For example, a young U.S. Navy ensign, Chester W. Nimitz, commanded a gunship in the Philippines during tense times between the US and Japan in 1907.[17] He probably never thought that he would become the Commander in Chief of the Pacific Fleet against the Imperial Japanese Navy roughly thirty-seven years later.[18] That same year, a West Point cadet was barely making the grades to graduate with his peers, but thirty-seven years later, Lieutenant General George S. Patton, Jr, commanded the newly activated Armored Corps in North Africa, Seventh Army in Sicily, and the Third Army in Normandy.[19] A young elementary aged boy, played like any other boy his age would, but thirty-seven years later, Lieutenant General James Doolittle was the Eighth Air Force Commanding General.[20] The careers and accomplishments of these three iconic leaders of World War II were all products of World War I and the interwar years. They gleaned from their personal experiences and lessons learned from World War I and the evolving technology of that day. The one novel concept introduced during this time was the idea of strategic bombing. The idea of fighting a war and rendering the enemy incapable of fighting without having to send in ground force was a strong consideration for senior decision makers. There still existed opposing opinions that thought that the strategic bombing concept was over simplifying how to wage and win future wars.

Military theorists such as Billy Mitchell and Alfred Mahan also began to affect the ideas of how best to employ air and naval power in times of war during the early part of the century. Mitchell presented arguments such as investing in airplanes and ordnance to win the next war without paying such a hefty price in American casualties. Mahan argued that a large navy would win the next war by having greater presence across the globe and taking the battle to the open seas to protect the homeland. The forward presence would also have an impact on other nations across the globe.

Another key part to developing, maintaining, and deploying any military force is the financial aspect. Postwar allied nations incurred a significant amount of debt that reflected in their decisions to delay modernizing the military. Democratic governments did not increase taxes, but they still modestly invested in the military in order to avoid being surprised by the next war.[21] Measuring the percentage of gross domestic product is one way to define how serious a nation is about investing in security. In terms of percentage of gross domestic product spending on their military in 1938, the democracies fell to fourth (Britain), fifth (United States) and sixth (France).[22] Conversely, Japan moved from last in military spending in 1933 to third in 1938 behind Germany and the Soviet Union.[23] This comparison of national military spending provides an early indication of Japanese intentions prior to World War II. The decision to assume away the option of a possible Japanese attack on the United States proved disastrous.

The Japanese attack on December 7, 1941 caught the United States by surprise and unprepared. Although Congress passed the National Defense Act of 1940, which increased the manpower of the Army and Army Air Corps, it also directed the acceleration of ship construction.[24] President Roosevelt also energized various appropriation bills, which directed the Navy to establish the Pacific Fleet in Pearl Harbor.[25] These legislative efforts were heading in the right direction as the country's leadership viewed the idea of entering the war as a matter of when they would enter the war not a matter if they would enter the war. The effects of implementing Congress' plan to manufacture military equipment took some time before assembly lines were mass-producing war material. The slow process was evident in "December of 1941, the United States had only forty-five modern fighter planes ready to fly on the Pacific coast."[26] After the devastating attack on Pearl Harbor, the United States was barely able to muster a division size force to fight the Japanese in the Pacific. This was of little concern to the Japanese as they defeated US forces on Wake and Guam and a few months later the Philippines. Additionally, the United States had a "Germany First" policy concerning the global conflict.[27] This meant that whatever scarce resources America had, would be committed to the European theater. The United States had limited resources and could not support two major theater engagements, but the military planners started looking for options. Even then, the United States was short escort ships in their initial support for the Allies in Europe.

Over a year after entering, a war that was going on its fourth year, the American and Free French forces outnumbered the Germans at Kasserine Pass. The Allies were surprised and then driven back several miles across the plains of Tunisia, while only suffering approximately one sixth of the casualties of the American and French forces. [28] The military once again rushed through training to deploy units to the fight and grew four times than it did for World War I. The total Active Duty personnel during World War II (1939-1946) exceeded sixteen million.[29] The magnitude of the conflict was enormous and military planners nor could anyone else have accurately predicted future conflicts. Better analysis and preparation during peacetime could reduce the number of reoccurring lessons that are relearned every time the United States enters a war. The American military recuperated from the initial battles and the military industrial complex produced and unprecedented amount of equipment, weapons and ammo for the fighting force. The United States persevered through these challenges and sacrificed many lives as they defeated the Axis nations.

The conclusion of America's war with Japan captured the attention of the entire world. The dropping of the atomic bomb would change the course of national strategy after World War II. President Harry Truman did not have a favorable opinion of large standing armies during peacetime. The introduction of the atomic bomb and capability to deliver via an Air Force platform reduced the importance of the land force because of this new advanced weapon.[30] The United States experienced a growth and reduction of the military and had a plan to do the same at the conclusion of World War II, but the plan failed. President Truman stated, "we will not measure up to [our] responsibilities by the simple return to normalcy."[31] His statement referenced the global responsibilities that were neglected after World War I and he did not want the country to return to isolationism. Within a year after the end of the war, 75 percent of the force returned to civilian life, the defense budget reduction was 50 percent the first year and reduced by 84 percent in 1947.[32] This amounted to a total force of approximately 1.4 million, which was the largest than any other American peacetime force.

Additionally, President Truman tried to unify the military service, which members of the Navy and some members of Congress opposed. The Navy preferred to keep things as they were with two separate service chiefs. This format created friction during the Pacific campaign of World War II, which Roosevelt handled, but President Truman did not want to be a referee between the Army and the Navy. Truman then recommended to Congress to have one civilian appointee to manage the Department of Defense.[33] This concept was a part of a major reorganization of the United States Department of Defense. The National Security Act of 1947, established a Secretary of Defense, created the United States Air Force, National Security

Council and the Central Intelligence Agency.[34] The reorganization inherited a great deal of

inter-service rivalry during the process. Lieutenant General Victor H. Krulak captures the

tension of that time:

> In time of peace, the armed services compete for dollars, in time of war they
> compete for military tasks and material priority. We find ourselves in competition
> all the time. Add to this the leavening of pride in your uniform and your service
> and you can see at once that there are the ingredients of a constant conflict. Now
> this conflict need not take virulent form but when dollars are hard to get or the
> tasks are subject of great competition it can become virulent as it has in the past.[35]

Each service was ruthlessly competing for their own existence by defending their relevance.

Instead of operating jointly, each service was concentrating on their own specialties. The Army

focused on the land component role, the Air Force was fixated on strategic bombers, and the

Navy was fixated on building a carrier fleet.[36]

The defense transformation was not the only aspect changing after World War II. The

world's security scene changed with the Soviet Union rising as the next formidable threat, which

started the era of the Cold War. The military still continued to mobilize and demobilize during

the Korean War and had to implement the draft to meet the manpower requirements. The draft

was another indication of the military not being adequately prepared. The challenge of mixing a

force of volunteer force with conscript calls for minimal training prior to deploying into a

combat zone. Again, the United States suffered staggering number of casualties by once again,

focusing on quantity and not quality. During both wars, approximately 100,000 died and over

400,000 wounded.[37] The continuous trend of growth and reduction proves ineffective and

inefficient to the readiness of the national defense of the United States. After Vietnam, the

military was "hollowed out" as it returned to an all-volunteer force, but the Soviet Union still

loomed on the horizon.[38] The United States could not afford to be unprepared if it was to face the Soviet Union. The Soviet threat was reason enough for the United States to maintain a large peacetime force.

The effective implementation of the national powers enabled the United States to achieve its objective without having to go to war. Following the end of the Cold War, the U.S. Armed Forces were already postured for the next threat in the Middle East. While the outcome was victorious, some argue that there was no contest, because "they [the Iraqis] were the most incompetent army in the world."[39] Despite an opinion of the enemy, that does not make the perceived threat any less formidable. However, one could ask if the outcome would have been different if the Gulf War took place in the mid-1990s after a period of force reduction. The fact that the military was prepared demonstrates the importance of having a peacetime force ready to face the next threat because no two wars are the same.

Strategy and Force Structure

Because the size and structure of our military and defense budget have to be driven by a strategy – not the other way around.[40]

- President Barak Obama

As the military prepares to transition security responsibilities to Iraq and Afghan security forces, the nation needs to ask, "what's next?" Interwoven in analyzing how to prepare for the next conflict is the global economic crisis. The situation invokes more questions than answers; however, some answers came in the form of the priorities outlined in the new strategic guidance for the Department of Defense.

The President directed former Secretary Gates to conduct a review of the military strategy in April 2011 and find ways to reduce defense spending by $400 billion over the next decade. This analysis provides much of the background for the strategic guidance presented on January 5, 2012. The President's initial directive to the Secretary of Defense became legislation through the recently passed Budget Control Act of 2011, which requires a reduction in federal spending and in particular the Department of Defense.[41] The President's comments and the 2012 strategic guidance both mention avoiding the previous mistakes made during force reductions within the Department of Defense. Instead, the reduction will be done responsibly, while maintaining necessary capabilities vital to our national defense.

The strategic guidance defines what the defense priorities are and shifts the military's focus from the Middle East to the Asia-Pacific region. Shifting the region of focus does not mean a total disregard to all the accomplishments in the Middle East. The shift recognizes China's strong influence in the region economically and militarily.[42] The goal is for American military forces to reengage the region through military exercises with partner nations and peacekeeping deployments in the Pacific while still maintaining a presence in regions such as the Middle East and other parts around the globe. Additionally, the Department of Defense identified that Europe is able to provide and maintain its own security, therefore reducing the need for such a large U.S. military presence in the continent.[43] This transition relieves the US forces of some of its tasks in the European theater in order to support the military's priorities elsewhere.

Over 95 percent of the world's commerce travels via water and it is paramount for these waterways to be safe and secure to allow freedom of movement to support international trade.[44] In the recent past, the world has seen the disruptive effects that piracy can have on commerce. A military presence along the sea lines of communication will aid in the prevention of such actions. The US economy and the global economy depend on open and secure sea-lanes for nations to operate and prosper. Such a responsibility cannot and should not be on one nation; instead it is important that partnerships develop among the members of the international community.

The new strategy deviates from a previous requirement to conduct two major conflicts in separate regions and relieves some of the burden from the service chiefs.[45] This concept lends itself to the reduction of land forces for both the Army and the Marine Corps. Many critics say that this is unacceptable and shows a sign of weakness to the global community. The Global War on Terrorism focused it resources in two countries in the Middle Eastern region as well as parts of Southwest Asia.

The last time a major two-theater war was fought occurred during World War II in the European and Pacific theaters. Defense Secretary Les Aspin first mentioned the major regional contingencies concept in 1993 in a Defense Bottom Up Review.[46] When Colin Powell served as the chairman of the Joint Chiefs, he presented the concept of fighting in one region and when another conflict emerges, the nation continues to deploy forces to address the second threat. The assumed risk is in minimizing the size of on operational reserve. This is not a strategy rather a capability, which continued to be briefed and presented as part of the national strategy for almost two decades.[47] Colin Powell also used the term "near-simultaneity." Mark Thompson from Time Magazine wrote, "that's not a word generals, or English speaking humans, regularly use. It means: *not at the same time*. It means close, as with horseshoes and nuclear weapons." This concept briefed well and was the platform used to maintain a larger than necessary peacetime force for several years. Although the military will not have the force to fight in two different regions, leaders have addressed the need for the military to operate in a new domain, the cyber domain.

Commanders traditionally conduct military operations in the air, land, sea and space domains. Future military operations will also include cyber operations to defend friendly networks, as well as exploit and attack enemy networks. Increasing the military's cyberwarfare capability is an increasing priority for the Department of Defense. The vast amount of information exchanged and store in the cyber domain has made it a vulnerable target for malicious even physically destructive actions. The Stuxnet worm that targeted Iran's nuclear facilities is one example at the enormous capabilities within the cyber domain. Just as sea-lanes are vital to commerce and trade, so is the cyber domain. This is such an integrated domain throughout all the elements of national power; each element must protect its information from malicious groups. The cyber world exceeds beyond the military's ability to influence; in conjunction with other government entities, the military is responsible to safeguard the information concerning national security with the .mil realm while the Department of Homeland Security manages the .gov sites.

The Department of Defense's strategic guidance sets the foundation to enable the military to be best prepared for the uncertainties of the 21st century. It outlines the priorities and then lists the ten primary missions of the U.S. Armed Forces:[48]

- Counter Terrorism and Irregular Warfare
- Deter and Defeat Aggression
- Project Power Despite Anti-Access/Area Denial Challenges
- Counter Weapons of Mass Destruction
- Operate Effectively in Cyberspace and Space
- Maintain a Safe, Secure, and Effective Nuclear Deterrent
- Defend the Homeland and Provide Support to Civil Authorities
- Provide a Stabilizing Presence
- Conduct Stability and Counterinsurgency Operations
- Conduct Humanitarian, Disaster Relief, and Other Operations

The initial mission list does not appear conducive to an actual reduction in force, but the Service Chiefs have the arduous task of finding the right size force to fulfill each the missions listed above. Historically, force reductions have been more of a knee jerk reaction with across the board cuts based on a number, but the right sized force will reduce the quantity while maintaining or perhaps even enhancing quality. Technology will continue to develop to

14

compliment the military and provide enablers to make the nation's military the best in the world. The President and the Secretary of Defense also emphasized the keys to accomplishing these missions are the joint force and international partners.

Critics are quick to call this a budget driven strategy, others argue that the cuts are not deep enough, but the focus must be on a balanced force able to defeat the next threat. The unofficial land component reduction is anticipated to be in the range to a 10-15 percent for both the Army and the Marine Corps. The decline in manpower is approximately 80,000 Soldiers and 20,000 Marines. That percentage range takes the Marine Corps numbers to pre-Iraq surge numbers of 2006. The Army would have roughly the same size force it did before 9/11. The critics seem to forget that the increase in military to support the surge intended to be temporary. After this round of budget cuts, the United States will spend more than the next ten countries on the defense budget. (Annex A)

America's Force in Readiness

A middleweight force, we are light enough to get there quickly, but heavy enough to carry the day upon arrival, and capable of operating independent of local infrastructure.[49]

- General James F. Amos, Commandant of the Marine Corps

On 22 October 2010 at Marine Barracks Washington, Secretary Gates welcomed General Amos as the 35th Commandant of the Marine Corps by challenging him "to think hard about their role after spending the past eight years fighting as a so-called second land army."[50] This was not a surprise to General Amos since he witnessed the beginnings of the defense budget cuts first hand in his previous billet as Assistant Commandant of the Marine Corps. He did not waste any time as the newly appointed Commandant and called for a Force Structure Review of the Marine Corps in the fall of 2010.[51] As the wars in Iraq and Afghanistan kept extending, debates occurred about the necessity of the Marine Corps amphibious capability because the Marines were looking more and more like a second land army. This immediately triggered the Marine Corps' senior leadership to defend the services unique capability. The concern then becomes one of relevance to the nation and distinction from the other services. When Marines hear a statement like that, Marines quickly remember the numerous fights for the existence of the Marine Corps throughout their history, which is captured in Victor Krulak's *First to Fight*. The purpose of the Force Structure Review was to ensure the Marine Corps is still relevant and to convince the civilian leadership that the Marine Corps is flexible and responsive enough to answer that nation's need. The Marine Corps had to prove that it is postured as "America's force in readiness" not only for the next conflict but also for the next 15 to 20 years.[52]

General Amos' initial guidance for the Force Structure Review Group was to define the role of the Marin Corps in the future joint environment.[53] A priority for Marines includes the return to their amphibious nature. This mission was not the Marine Corps priority during the long war in Iraq and Afghanistan. The Marine Corps will not dismiss the lessons learned over the last ten years but incorporate them to add to their relevance in the 21st century. Shifting the focus to the Asia-Pacific region is a perfect fit for the Navy-Marine Corps team and helps remind the services their history and will continue to have relevance in the future.

First, the definition of the Marine Corps' role with the Joint Force is:[54]

- An integrated and balanced air-ground logistics team
- Forward deployed and forward engaged – ever ready to respond and protest as directed
- Responsive and scalable – ready today to respond to the full range of crises and contingencies
- Trained and equipped to Integrate with other Services, Allies and Interagency partners
- The USMC is a Middleweight Force… "light enough to get there quickly, heavy enough to carry the day upon arrival"

Identifying the Marine Corps role established the framework for the Commandant to brief the Secretaries of the Navy and Defense and for the review group to identify the capabilities necessary to accomplish them.[55] The challenge now becomes matching the capabilities with a force structure that is integrated, balanced, responsive, scalable, and affordable for the nation. That then led to a capabilities-based review across the entire force of active, reserve, and civilian components. The detailed refinement included comparing the force with existing OPLANS and a Red Cell within the review group to challenge the feasibility of the recommended force structure.[56]

The results of the Force Structure Review Group recommend that manpower reduces its ranks by 15,200 Marines; from 202,000 to 186,800 while the reserve component remains at 39,600 Marines.[57] The reduction is not equal across the service; instead the review group recommended a reorganization of the service. This will ensure that it "is not simply a reduced version of today's Marine Corps nor is it a reversion to the pre-9/11 posture."[58] The critical analysis applied to the restructuring of the Marine Corps is evidence of not wanting to repeat previous mistakes instead the Marine Corps is restructuring with a vision towards future conflicts.

Several of the initiatives implemented in the restructure involve having units manned at high states of readiness closer to 95-99 percent instead of the former 60-80 percent that would have to be augmented by other units in order to meet operational commitments. Another initiative includes flattening out commands by reducing redundant command structures that are no longer necessary with a smaller force. Increases came in the areas of Marine Special Operations Command (MARSOC) and Marine Corps Cyberspace Command (MARFORCYBER) to prepare for future contingencies.

Finally, the realignment of five regionally focused command elements structures within the component commands will facilitate the rapid crisis response capability allowing for a scalable Marine Air Ground Task Force (MAGTF). For example, Marine Corps Forces Pacific Command (MARFORPAC) will have the personnel to create a command element for a MAGTF to respond to a crisis in that region and the MAGTF will fall in under a Marine Expeditionary Brigade command structure. This previously was comprised of individual augments to make the command element, which affected the unit readiness of the sending units. The advantages of the newer model are continuity within the command and a staff that is already familiar with the region and its potential hot spots.[59]

These changes are a clear example of an institution that treasures its heritage and is able to maintain it while still being relevant today and for the uncertain future. The Marine Corps studies its own history and that of the nation to understand the adaptability necessary to continue to be "America's Expeditionary Force-in-Readiness."[60]

Conclusion

To be prepared for war is one of the most effectual means of preserving peace.[61]

- George Washington

During the summer of 2011, the Service Secretaries were given notice of the impending budget cuts and the time to conduct a thorough internal review of their respective services. Contrary to what the media expected and what is historically documented, there is no evidence of inter-service rivalry as was seen post World War II with the revolt of the admirals. In fact, the complete opposite happened and Service Chiefs are working together to accomplish the goal of continuing to be the world's finest fighting force. On two occasions, Service Chiefs admitted to meeting together to agree that there will not be any infighting made public. If there are disagreements, they are to handle it among themselves in private with the Chairman of the Joint Chiefs, arrive at a solution and move on.[62] This is a generation of leaders looking beyond their service and work together to jointly meet the challenges of the uncertain future.

"An early lead, or having triumphed in the last conflict, by no means guarantees success in coping with the sort of fundamental changes in future wars that now appear to lie just over the horizon, just out of clear view."[63] The task of implementing military form in the 21st century must not be business as usual, instead a very thorough analysis of current and future threats coupled with an intellectual and calculated rigor to design a balanced force necessary to meet the demand of an uncertain future. The preliminary actions presented so far, set the framework to restructure the military display solid evidence of dedicating the attention required to accomplish this task successfully. The approach of our civilian and military leadership actually does look at history and learns from our nation's past in order to provide a more secure and prosperous future for the nation and its allies throughout the globe. Additionally, the reduction in force will foster a joint requirement as well as an interagency requirement to provide the whole of government approach in facing a wide spectrum of challenges. The 21st century has changed dramatically and when defense resources are limited and security demands increase, the solution is a balanced force across the military services, interagency participation and international partnership to ensure security and prosperity across the globe.

Endnotes

[1] http://www.alberteinsteinsite.com/quotes/einsteinquotes.html

[2] http://www.reagan.utexas.edu/archives/speeches/1983/32383d.htm

[3] Richard K. Betts, *Military Readiness: Concepts, Choices, Consequencs* (Washington: Brookings Institute, 1995), 5.

[4] David Cartwright, A Historical Commentary on Thucydides (Michigan: University of Michigan Press:1997) ,114.

[5] William G. Anderson, *The Price of Liberty: The Public Debt of the American Revolution* (Charlottesville: University of Virginia:1983) 3.

[6] Robert D. Hormats, *The Price of Liberty: Paying for America's Wars*, (New York: Henry Holt and Company, 2007), XII.

[7] Charles E. Heller, ed. *America's First Battles 1776-1965*, (Lawrence, Kansas: UniversityPress of Kansas,1986), 2.

[8] Clint Rossiter, ed. *The Federalist Papers*. (New York: Signet Classic, 2003) 535.

[9] Heller, 37.

[10] Ibid, 59.

[11] Ibid, 87.

[12] James F. Dunnigan and Raymond M. Macedonia, *Getting it Right: American Military Reforms After Vietnam to the Persian Gulf and Beyond*. (New York: William Morrow and Company, 1993), 26.

[13] James F. Dunnigan and Raymond M Macedonia, 26.

[14] Heller, 150-156.

[15] Ibid, 157.

[16] William Murray and Allan R. Millet, ed. *Military Innovation in the Interwar Period*. (New York: Cambridge University Press, 1998), 3.

[17] Ibid, 329.

[18] Ibid, 329.

[19] Ibid, 330.

[20] Ibid, 330.

[21] Ibid, 333.

[22] Ibid, 333.

[23] Ibid, 334.

[24] Hormats, 139.

[25] Ibid,

[26] James F. Dunnigan and Raymond M Macedonia, 42.

[27] Richard Frank, *Guadalcanal: The Definative Account of the Landmark Battle*. (New York: Penguin Books, 1990), 6.

[28] James F. Dunnigan and Raymond M Macedonia, 42.

[29] Anne LeLand and Mari-Jana Oboroceanu, *American War and Military Operations Casualties: Lists and Statistics*, CRS Report for Congress RL32492 (Washington, DC: Congressional Research Service, February 26, 2010. 2.

[30] James F. Dunnigan and Raymond M Macedonia, 50.

[31] Hormats, 175

[32] James F. Dunnigan and Raymond M Macedonia, 51.

[33] LtGen Victor Krulak, *First to Fight*, (Annapolis: Naval Institute Press, 1999), 120-122.

[34] http://intelligence.senate.gov/nsaact1947.pdf

[35] LtGen Victor Krulak , Oral History Transcript (Washington DC: Historical Division, HQMC, 1973) 113-114.

[36] James F. Dunnigan and Raymond M Macedonia, 54.

[37] Anne LeLand and Mari-Jana Oboroceanu, 3.

[38] James F. Dunnigan and Raymond M Macedonia, 97.

[39] Thomas Withington, What If We Battled a Real Army?" Long Island Newsday, August 27,2003, quoted in Winslow T. Wheeler and Lawrence J. Korb, "Military Reform: An Uneven History and an Uncertain Future", (Stanford, California: Stanford University Press, 2009),93.

[40] President Barak Obama, "Remarks on Military Spending" (speech, Department of Defense, Arlington , VA, January 5, 2012)

[41] Ibid

[42] Department of Defense, Sustaining U.S. Global Leadership, Priorities for 21st Century Defense (Washington, DC: Department of Defense, 2012). January 5, 2012. http://www.defense.gov/news/Defense_Strategic_Guidance.pdf.

[43] Ibid

[44] General James Amos, "America's Expeditionary Force in Readiness" (lecture, Marine Corps University, Quantico, VA, January 4, 2012).

[45] Department of Defense, Sustaining U.S. Global Leadership, Priorities for 21st Century Defense (Washington, DC: Department of Defense, 2012). January 5, 2012. http://www.defense.gov/news/Defense_Strategic_Guidance.pdf.

[46] Department of Defense, "Report on Bottom Up Review" October 1993 http://www.rand.org/content/dam/rand/pubs/monograph_reports/MR1387/MR1387.ch3.pdf, 48.

[47] Mark Thompson, "The Two-MRC Strategy: Major Regional Contingencies, or Mythical Routine Canards?" Time, January 4, 2012,: http://battleland.blogs.time.com/2012/01/04/the-two-mrc-strategy-major-regional-contingencies-or-mythical-routine-canards/#ixzz1k2dEDIOa (accessed January 5, 2012.)

[48] Sustaining U.S. Global Leadership, *Priorities for 21st Century Defense* (Washington, DC: Department of Defense, 2012).

[49] Reshaping America's Expeditionary Force in Readiness, *Report of the 2010 Marine Corps Force Structure Review Group* (Quantico, VA: Marine Corps Combat Development Command, 2010).

[50] Sandra Erwin, post on" Gates Tells Gen. Amos: 'Think Hard' About the Marine Corps' Future Role" National Defense Magazine comment posted October 22, 2010, http://www.nationaldefensemagazine.org/blog/Lists/Posts/Post.aspx?ID=223

[51] David S. Clouds, "Defense chief Gates orders review of Marines' role," August 12, 2010 http://article.latimes.com/2010/aug/12/world/la-fg-gates-speech-20100813

[52] Reshaping America's Expeditionary Force in Readiness, *Report of the 2010 Marine Corps Force Structure Review Group* (Quantico, VA: Marine Corps Combat Development Command, 2010).

[53] J.R.Wilson, "Defining the Future of the Marine Corps," October 11, 2011 http://www.defensemedianetwork.com/stories/defining-the-future-marine-corps/

[54] Reshaping America's Expeditionary Force in Readiness, *Report of the 2010 Marine Corps Force Structure Review Group* (Quantico, VA: Marine Corps Combat Development Command, 2010).

[55] J.R.Wilson, "Defining the Future of the Marine Corps," October 11, 2011 http://www.defensemedianetwork.com/stories/defining-the-future-marine-corps/

[56] Reshaping America's Expeditionary Force in Readiness, *Report of the 2010 Marine Corps Force Structure Review Group* (Quantico, VA: Marine Corps Combat Development Command, 2010).

[57] Ibid

[58] Ibid

[59] Kevin Baron, *Joint Chiefs Line Up To Defend Budget Contraction*, January 30, 2012 http://m100group.wordpress.com/2012/01/31/joint-chiefs-line-up-to-defend-budget-contraction-by-kevin-baron/

[60] Reshaping America's Expeditionary Force in Readiness, *Report of the 2010 Marine Corps Force Structure Review Group* (Quantico, VA: Marine Corps Combat Development Command, 2010).

[61] http://www.law.ou.edu/ushistory/washsu.shtml, first State of the Union Address

[62] General Norton A, Schwartz (USAF) and General James Amos (USMC) commented on the services working together more than ever and strengthen cooperative relationships during the defense budget cuts. Service Chief Lectures (Marine Corps University, Quantico, VA, December 2011 and January 2012)

[63] William Murray and Allan R. Millet, 414.

[64] Anup Shah, *World Military Spending*, May 2, 2011, http://www.globalissues.org/article/75/world-military-spending

[65] *Defense Costs,* June 8th 2011, 14:00 by The Economist online http://www.economist.com/blogs/dailychart/2011/06/military-spending

Bibliography

Anderson, William G. *The Price of Liberty: The Public Debt of the American Revolution.* Charlottesville: University of Virginia:1983

Baron, Kevin *Joint Chiefs Line Up To Defend Budget Contraction*, National Journal Daily, January 30, 2012 http://m100group.wordpress.com/2012/01/31/joint-chiefs-line-up-to-defend-budget-contraction-by-kevin-baron/ (accessed February 1, 2012).

Betts, Richard K. *Military Readiness: Concepts, Choices, Consequences.* Washington, DC: Brookings Institute, 1995.

Brasher, Bart *Implosion : Downsizing the U.S. Military, 1987-2015.* Westport, CT : Greenwood Press, 2000.

Cartwright, David. *A Historical Commentary on Thucydides.* Michigan: University of Michigan Press, 1997.

Clouds, David S. *"Defense chief Gates orders review of Marines' role,"* *LATimes.com*, August 12, 2010 http://article.latimes.com/2010/aug/12/world/la-fg-gates-speech-20100813 (accessed December 18, 2011).

Davidson, Michael W., *Victory at Risk: Restoring America's Military Power.* Minneapolis, MN: Zenith Press, 2009.

Department of Defense, *Sustaining U.S. Global Leadership, Priorities for 21st Century Defense.* January 5, 2012. http://www.defense.gov/news/DefenseStrategicGuidance.pdf.

Dunnigan, James F. and Raymond M. Macedonia. *Getting it Right: American Military Reforms After Vietnam to the Persian Gulf and Beyond.* New York: William Morrow and Company, Inc. 1993.

Durenberger, David. *Neither Madmen Nor Messiahs A Policy of National Security for America.* Minneapolis, Minnesota: Piranha Press, 1984.

Eland, Ivan. *Putting Defense Back into U.S. Defense Policy.* Westport, CT: Praeger Publishers, 2001.

Erwin, Sandra. "Gates Tells Gen. Amos: 'Think Hard' About the Marine Corps' Future Role" *National Defense Magazine,* October 22, 2010, http://www.nationaldefensemagazine.org/blog/Lists/Posts/Post.aspx?ID=223 (accessed December 17, 2011).

Frank, Richard. Guadalcanal: The Definitive Account of the Landmark Battle. New York: Penguin Books, 1990.

Headquarters Marine Corps. *Reshaping America's Expeditionary Force in Readiness*, Report of the 2010 Marine Corps Force Structure Review Group Quantico, VA: Marine Corps Combat Development Command, 2010.

Heller, Charles E. and William A. Stofft. *America's First Battles, 1776-1965*. Kansas: University Press of Kansas.

Hormats, Robert D., *The Price of Liberty: Paying for America's Wars from the Revolution to the War on Terror,* New York: Henry Holt and Company, 2007.

Krulak, Victor H., *First to Fight*. Annapolis: Naval Institute Press, 1999.

Krulak, Victor H. Oral History Transcript. Washington, D.C.: Historical Division, HQMC, 1973.

LeLand, Anne and Mari-Jana Oboroceanu, *American War and Military Operations Casualties: Lists and Statistics*, CRS Report for Congress RL32492 Washington, DC: Congressional Research Service, February 26, 2010.

Martin, Aaron L. "Paying for War: Funding U.S. Military Operations Since 2001." Doctoral dissertation, RAND Graduate School, 2011. http://merln.ndu.edu

Murray, Williamson and Allan R. Millett, ed. *Military Innovation in the Interwar Period*. New York: Cambridge University Press, 1996.

Obama, Barak. "Remarks on Military Spending" Speech, Department of Defense, Arlington, VA January 5, 2012.

Rossiter, Clint, ed. The Federalist Papers. New York: Signet Classic, 2003.

Thompson, Mark "The Two-MRC Strategy: Major Regional Contingencies, or Mythical Routine Canards?" *Time*, January 4, 2012,: http://battleland.blogs.time.com/2012/01/04/the-two-mrc-strategy-major-regional-contingencies-or-mythical-routine-canards/#ixzz1k2dEDIOa (accessed January 5, 2012)

Wheeler, Winslow T., ed. *America's Defense Meltdown*: *Pentagon reform for President Obama and the new Congress*. Stanford: Stanford Security Studies, 2009.

Wilson, J.R. "Defining the Future of the Marine Corps," October 11, 2011 http://www.defensemedianetwork.com/stories/defining-the-future-marine-corps/ (accessed December 18, 2011).

Withington, Thomas. *What If We Battled a Real Army?*. Long Island Newsday, August 27,2003, quoted in Winslow T. Wheeler and Lawrence J. Korb, "Military Reform: An Uneven History and an Uncertain Future", Stanford, California: Stanford University Press, 2009:93.